Jordan's World

The Boy Who Proved Them Wrong

Written by Jordan Christian LeVan

Illustrated by Isabella Millet

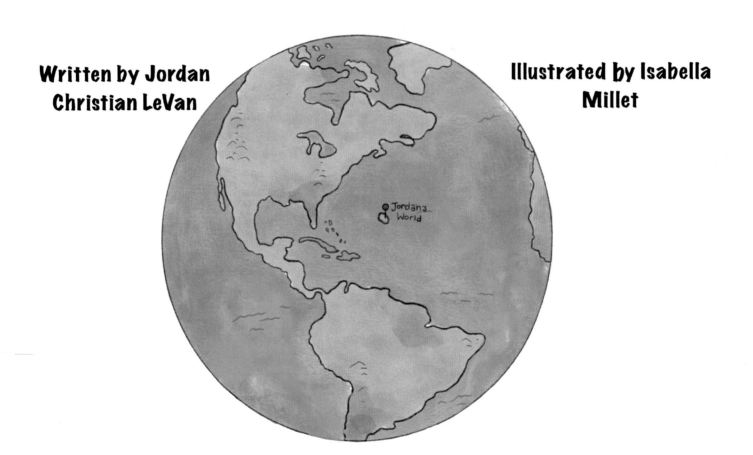

Jordan's World

The Boy Who Proved Them Wrong

Written by Jordan
Christian LeVan

Illustrated by
Isabella Millet

Author Biography

Jordan Christian LeVan is an apraxia, disability, and mental health advocate. He graduated in the year 2020 with his Bachelor of Arts in Psychology, focusing on Mental Health, from Guilford College in Greensboro, North Carolina. Jordan runs a blog called *Fighting for my Voice: My Life with Verbal Apraxia*, where he gives people an inside view on what it's like to live with Verbal Apraxia. Jordan is an advocate, blogger, motivational speaker, mentor, and author.

fightingformyvoice.com
Facebook.com/fightingformyvoice

Acknowledgments

Author: Jordan Christian LeVan
Illustrator: Isabella Millet
Editor: Lindsay LeVan Townsend

Welcome back to Jordan's World, a non-fiction book series with stories of my life as a child in the form of art. This story is about my speech-language pathologist who told me I would never speak on my own.

I want to dedicate this book to my mom. I love you, and thank you for fighting for my voice until I could on my own. Thank you for always being my rock, and advocating for me. I learned from the best. I want to thank everybody in my life who loves and supports me. Also, thank you to my child self for blocking out the background noise and staying strong. Here is my story.

The leaves were falling and starting to change colors. Jordan didn't know about the war that was coming this autumn.

It was a rough few months, but not just with the weather changing. Jordan was going to speech therapy and fighting for his voice daily.

The school speech therapist came to Jordan's classroom to pick him up and take him to speech therapy. He walked through the halls with her, preparing for the battle.

Jordan walked back to his classroom and sat beside his best friend named Linwood.

Later in the school day, Jordan's mom came to eat lunch with him. She brought him lunch to school.

Jordan put down his head to go into his own world, a place he dreamed of, where inclusion was part of the outside world.

12

"Jordan has apraxia. He knows what he wants to say, but sometimes he can't get the words out," Jordan's mom told his classmates.

13

Jordan's mom got in touch with the people she needed to reach, and she wasn't afraid to say what was needed on repeat.

18

The speech therapist then teamed up with Jordan to make sure his voice would never fade away.

Although Jordan's World was safe and secure, he still wanted to be part of the outside world.

He just wanted everybody to be loved and accepted for who they are.

22

They said Jordan would never speak on his own, but now Jordan knows their words never held any truth.

23

Despite what others had said, Jordan found himself in the daylight again.

He learned that apraxia wasn't a bad thing after all. It turned out to be one of his greatest strengths, and he proved them all wrong.

A Letter to My
Younger Self:

Dear Jordan,
I know other people's words hurt, and I want to let you know your feelings are completely valid. With your speech difference being rare, I know you don't have any representation. You look around you and see other people's speech come so effortlessly. So, you think, "Why me?" The reason you have verbal apraxia is unknown, and I know it's hard for you to accept it. But one day, Jordan, you will. I want you to know things get better, and no, not in that cheesy way they say in the commercials.

You learn to accept and love yourself for everything that makes you who you are. You will grow up and one day be the representation for verbal apraxia because you won't want anybody to feel alone like you did. I'm so proud of you for fighting for your voice.

You are going to turn what others consider your weakness into one of your biggest strengths. If the adults around you knew your ability to believe you're capable of anything; they would have feared your determination.
Love,
Jordan Christian

Thank you for visiting Jordan's World. Remember, what you say can affect and stay with a person for the rest of their life. Be cautious of what you say. And no matter what is said to you, remember you have the strength and power to rise above. Nobody can predict your future. The following pages have surprise gifts for you. You will need a trusted adult's help.

Much love,
Jordan Christian

Jordan's  World

CERTIFICATE OF RECOGNITION

Given To

_____

for fighting for their voice.

Image of the Honoree

Official Fighting For My Voice Member

_____

"My passion gave me power."

Jordan Christian

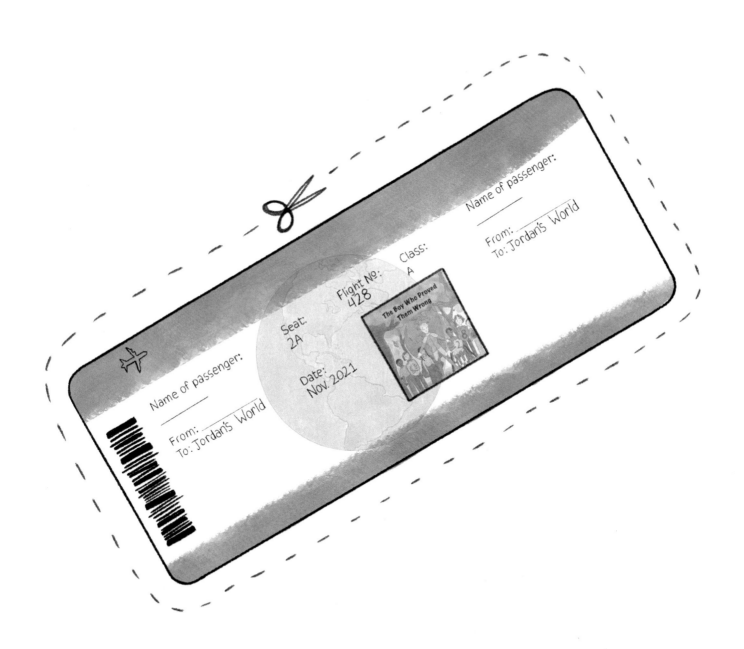

Name of passenger:
_____
From: _____
To: Jordan's World

Seat:
2A

Flight No:
428

Class:
A

Date:
Nov. 2021

The Boy Who Proved Them Wrong

Name of passenger:
_____
From: _____
To: Jordan's World

This book was Illustrated by Isabella Millet. To see more of her work or connect with Isabella, visit her at isabellamillet.com